B890

GOVERNMENT

Prepared for the course team by Allan Plath and Monir Tayeb
with contributions by John Drew

MBA

International Enterprise

The Open University

BUSINESS SCHOOL

OPEN UNIVERSITY COURSE TEAM

Core Group

Dr Allan Plath, *Course Team Chair*
Mr Jon Billsberry, *Critical Reader*
Mr Martin Brazier, *Designer*
Mr Eric Cassells, *Author*
Dr Timothy Clark, *Author*
Ms Karen Dolan, *Course Manager*
Mrs Shirley Eley, *Course Team Assistant*
Ms Ann Faulkner, *Liaison Librarian*
Ms Julie Fletcher, *Editor*
Mr Mike Green, *Critical Reader*
Mrs Cherry Harris, *Course Team Assistant*
Dr Nick Heap, *Author*
Mr Roy Lawrance, *Graphic Artist*
Dr Richard Mole, *Production Director, OUBS*
Prof. Derek Pugh, *Author*
Prof. Janette Rutterford, *Author*
Ms Linda Smith, *Project Controller*
Prof. Andrew Thomson, *Author*
Mr Steve Wilkinson, *BBC Series Producer*

External consultants

Dr Jim Attridge, *Critical Reader*
Dr David Barnes, *Author*

Prof. Peter Dicken, *Author*
Prof. John Drew, *Author and Editor of the Reader*
Prof. Nigel Grimwade, *Author*
Prof. Malcolm Hill, *Author*
Prof. Paul Iles, *Author*
Mr Ian McCall, *Author*
Dr David Silk, *Author*
Dr Steve Tallman, *Author*
Prof. Monir Tayeb, *Author*

Developmental testers

Ms Barbara Awuku-Asabre
Mr Ian Cooley
Dr Alan Eggleston
Mr David Milton
Mr Roy Needham
Mr Fred Thomson

External assessors

Prof. Dr Pervez N. Ghauri, *University of Groningen, The Netherlands*
Prof. Simon Coke, *Edinburgh University Management School, Edinburgh*

The Open University, Walton Hall, Milton Keynes MK7 6AA

First published 1995, second edition 1999. Reprinted 1999, 2001

Edited, designed and typeset by The Open University.

Printed in the United Kingdom by Selwood Printing Ltd., Burgess Hill, West Sussex.

ISBN 0 7492 7679 7

For further information on Open University Business School courses and the Certificate, Diploma and MBA programmes, please contact the Course Sales Development Centre, The Open University, PO Box 222, Walton Hall, Milton Keynes MK7 6YY (Telephone: 01908 653449).

oubs.open.ac.uk

2.3

19041B/b890govui2.3

CONTENTS

INTRODUCTION

BACKGROUND TO THE UNIT

We have argued throughout the course so far that the world of international enterprise is complex. Mass communication media, fast and far-reaching transport systems, and satellite-based telecommunications are bringing the peoples and institutions of the world closer and closer. Firms that cross borders play a significant part in this complex world. They not only move goods and services from one country to another, they also influence the transformation of societies along the way.

Activities such as formulating policies and strategies, dealing with competitors, responding to customers' needs, coping with pressure groups, complying with government policies and regulations, designing appropriate organizational structures, and operating with appropriate technologies are among the normal preoccupations of managers in any organization. These are magnified and become far more complicated as companies stretch their boundaries to cover more and more countries.

This unit focuses on the ways in which organizations interact with governments. Big companies frequently have a department dedicated to this complex area of relations. These are sometimes known as corporate affairs or corporate communications departments. Managers in them will be skilled in strategy and government relations, in public relations and communications, in relations with the media and investors. Corporate affairs departments work closely in support of top management, often the chairman or a senior director, who will be chief spokesman for the company.

This is not to say that *all* activities related to the government in a firm are undertaken by a corporate affairs department. Even in large firms, managers 'on the ground' often have significant interactions with governmental bodies. Many of you will sit on technical and regulatory committees of various industry-wide or governmentally sponsored bodies and all managers will, at some time or another come into contact with the outcomes of the process of regulation. In smaller firms, each and every manager becomes a member of the 'corporate affairs team'. Thus, an understanding of the issues raised in this unit are key to effective long-term performance for all managers.

But note here that national and international politics are relevant to business organizations *only to the extent that their operations are affected by them*. Companies survive and flourish under conditions of relative stability and predictability. Instability, whether political or of any other kind, can often be a source of risk and threat that companies try to avoid, or at least reduce.

Political instability can also create opportunities for companies. Armies, it is said, march on their stomachs, but more often than not they would come to a complete halt if they did not have computers and copiers, radios and electronic communications. Companies, therefore, can find themselves supplying directly or indirectly these goods and facilities, both to official governments and perhaps to rebel governments seeking to overthrow them. Again, the judgement of what goods and spares can and cannot be supplied is a delicate one. Companies want to sell their goods and services, but they have to be extremely careful not to be seen to be meddling in politics, and it is not in their interest to do so. Company procedures and ethical codes are also part of the corporate affairs responsibility, not necessarily to define them, which is the task of senior management, but certainly to be involved in drawing them up.

Depending on the circumstances, political events can be considered as having both positive and negative consequences for the organizations involved. Viewed in this light, an important issue for managers is their ability to understand, predict and influence those actions taken by the state or by other political institutions and pressure groups in the host countries in which they operate. This unit is about helping you do just this.

AIMS AND OBJECTIVES

The unit's main aims are to:
- Point out the diversity of the political institutions that exist in the environment of the international enterprise.
- Emphasize the importance of the international political environment.
- Identify some of the major political institutions and forces that lie behind the events that affect organizations' strategies and operations.
- Examine the ways in which companies can work with governments to their mutual advantage.

When you have completed this unit, you should be able to:
- View the global environment with an increased awareness of and sensitivity to national political diversity.
- Understand the implications of local and global political events for organizations.
- Understand the universal nature of governments.
- Apply analytical techniques aimed at improving your company's decision-making processes with respect to political action.
- Understand the ways in which your company can exercise political influence.
- Understand the ways in which issue monitoring can help your company to respond better to changes in the political climate of a given country.

OVERVIEW OF THE UNIT

In Section 1 of this unit, we develop a framework that can be used to help you put the diversity of political systems and forces in the world into context. In this section, you will see that governments, no matter what their ideological complexion, have much in common. Through seeing the common features, we will begin to move towards a system of analysis of these political systems. Also in Section 1, we will see that the international enterprise has stakeholders who can bring pressure to bear upon it, and who must be accounted for in the decision-making process of the firm. Finally in this section, we develop the argument that the company/ country relationship is not one-sided. International enterprises need not adopt a passive attitude towards governmental action. They have power of their own and, in theory, can exercise this power.

Section 2 goes into more detail and focuses on the kinds of governmental activity that can create threats and opportunities for an international enterprise. Two aspects of this topic are discussed. The first is the relationships between governments and companies. The second is the efforts that nations have made at both global and regional levels to reduce uncertainty in the market and to enhance the flow of goods and services between countries.

Section 3 discusses the ways in which firms relate to the political environment. This section focuses on techniques for understanding the political environment, strategies for buffering the company from risk and, finally, ways of influencing governmental decision makers.

1 POLITICS: A FRAMEWORK

You may want to read the article in the course reader by Campanella, 'The effects of globalization and turbulence on policy-making processes'.

You would probably agree that little of what companies do, or the manner in which it is done, is guaranteed to escape governmental or political influence. In a given country some of this influence is routine. For example, all countries have regulations concerning the issuing of work permits for nationals of foreign countries. Many companies rotate significant sections of their labour forces around the world (for reasons discussed in the People unit). These companies need to take account of local rules and regulations, which can be time-consuming.

Virtually all areas of an organization's activities are affected by governmental action. Broadly speaking, political action can have consequences for all aspects of an organization's activities. In particular, we can think of political activity having influence over the following four areas:

1 overall planning and strategy making – for example, where to go and which countries to avoid, when to go to a foreign country, when to pull out

2 operational decisions – for example, nature and scope of operations, choice of production technology, raising funds for investment

3 interface activities – for example, negotiations (with governments, with trade partners), advertising, marketing

4 internal organization – for example, personnel selection and other staffing policies, human resource management.

In this section, we develop the argument that the international political scene can best be understood and analysed if we view political actors as stakeholders of the firm. We help you to understand the various functions that all governments must perform as stakeholders, and also to view the ideology of the government in two dimensions: participation and role. We point out that other groups are also active in the political environment of a company that operates in more than one country. These regional and global organizations have influence on the activities of companies. Finally, this section suggests that the power inherent in the relationships with political stakeholders is not one-sided. Firms as well as countries have power, and the outcome of negotiations is often compromise.

1.1 STAKEHOLDERS AND THE FIRM

One way of thinking about the influence of politics on the activities of international enterprise is the notion that all organizations have 'stakeholders', and must respond to the interests of their stakeholders. Each of a company's stakeholders has their own influence on the governments of the host countries in which the company operates. These stakeholders can, and sometimes do, influence the political and regulatory climate underlying the legislative and political acts of the host country.

The notion of the stakeholder is often associated with the philosophy of business ethics. It plays a particularly important role, however, in allowing managers to assess which groups have an interest in the company and which have the potential to influence the ways in which the company meets its long-term goals. By definition, stakeholders are groups who meet these criteria. This definition also has within it the roots of analysis for the manager. What managers must do is simply stated (although not so simply done): it is to identify who is interested in the company's activities and who can also influence the company in the pursuit of its goals. A simple model of some types of stakeholder is shown in Figure 1.

Note from this figure that there are two circles of groups that impinge on the company. The inner circle contains groups who are directly involved with the company, and with whom managers are likely to be in contact on a regular basis. These stakeholders are, by their very nature, likely to be taken into account in the decision-making processes of the firm. They are visible and often quite vocal. Organizations in the outer circle, however, often have a more subtle, indirect and diffuse potential for influencing the firm.

It is these 'outer ring' stakeholders that impinge upon the company politically. Figure 1 shows that among these stakeholders are governments (home and host), international bodies, and pressure groups. The media and public opinion are also included. Each one of these groups has its own special interest in the operations of the firm, and is likely to attempt to influence it. It is particularly important to understand governments, as they are the most likely to influence the company's actions.

Figure 1   Possible stakeholders of an international enterprise

1.2   THE NATURE OF GOVERNMENTS

Similarities in governmental structures

In the introduction to the course we argued that the cultural values of a nation can translate themselves into specific governmental structures. National culture is but one small part of the reason for the diversity of political systems in countries around the world. A detailed exploration of the reasons for diversity in governments is beyond the scope of this course but other forces driving this diversity include the history of a country, the degree of nationalism in a country, the geography of the country, the ethnicity of the nation and crude political opportunism.

The apparent diversity of governmental types in the world may lead you to think that they share little common ground. While this may be true, there are common features in the structures of all governments. It will be much easier for a manager to advise the company on government relations if he or she has a clear view of how the government in the host country operates. We use the word 'government' to cover a wide variety of organizations through which the government of a country carries out its responsibilities. The role and functions of these organizations need to be clearly understood if a company wants to monitor activities of importance to its operations and perhaps contribute to the debate on future legislation which might affect it. Figure 2 illustrates one way of looking at them.

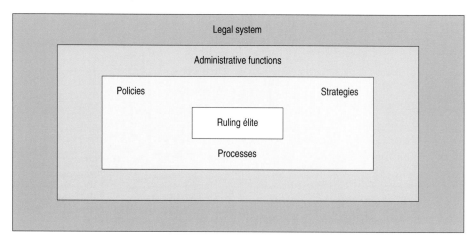

Figure 2   Government structures

This figure shows us that governments have, at their core, a group of people who rule the nation. This group can be a small cabal or can consist of many people. This ruling élite will have *strategies* for what they are trying to accomplish while ruling the nation. They will adopt *policies* (laws and regulations) and *processes* by which they exercise their power. No ruling élite can govern without structures to carry out *administrative functions*. There will be ministries, departments, agencies, quasi-statal organizations and the like through which the government exercises its rule. Finally, a mechanism for dispute resolution is necessary. This is the *legal system*. For now, it is important to note that, within the bounds of the dimensions just discussed, each national government structures itself in its own unique way. In order to work effectively for their company's interest, managers must be familiar with the governmental structure in each country in which they operate.

Activity 1

Think about your own country and choose a large foreign multinational company that has operations in it. Imagine you have been appointed as a government affairs consultant with them. How would you help its managers to identify the broad government structure of your country? Where would they get this information from? Which ministries would they need to know about? What level of government officials, if any, should they meet? What government agencies would be important to them? How could they legitimately influence the application of current legislation or the drawing up of future legislation that might affect them? Who would it be useful for them to know? How would they go about getting to know them? Who could make the introductions for them? What should they read? Should they hire a consultant to help them on a long-term basis, or invite a former government official or politician to join their board of directors?

What trade associations should they join? How could they show that their company was a good citizen? Remember that the company may have expatriate managers from its home country working in your country, as well as nationals of your country and perhaps some from other countries. Who is likely to be best at representing the company to your government? Will it be the chief executive or chairman, or will it depend on his or her nationality? Would it be better to meet with a senior director from the home country, or is it better for the company to have an image of being a local company? As there is limited time available, what is it essential to do as opposed to being nice to do? Are any stakeholders helpful in developing good relations with the government?

DTi

Environment

HBS

Transport (DETR)

Social Security

Local MP

TSD

Comment

You will have identified politicians and political parties, government officials and government ministers that the company should get to know. What about the level? How easy is it to meet them? What would be the purpose? Is it to promote the image of the company as a good citizen, which is important in itself, or is it to ensure that there is a good and continuing dialogue between the government and the foreign company? It is important to have good contacts with local members of parliament where the company factories or offices are located. The strategies of the government are implemented through policies and processes. Did you explain how they can best be monitored? What about contacts with the administration? Which government officials would it be worth keeping in contact with?

Are there government agencies to contact? What about the embassy of the home country? One of their most important jobs is to help companies understand the national political and economic environment. In certain circumstances, they will make contacts and, indeed, accompany your representatives from Head Office to meetings, if there are important bilateral issues involved such as double taxation agreements, investment incentives or government contracts to be won.

Are there trade associations or chambers of commerce in your country which the company should join? What about training courses or seminars? Do any of the foreign home-country managers speak your language? Should they be encouraged to do so?

The point we are making in this activity is a broad one. We suggest that you cannot understand governmental decision making without understanding governmental structure. Section 2 of this unit explores issues related to working with the various parts of government to achieve mutual advantage.

A final point must be made here. The process of government is not simple. A variety of political actors have roles. Too often, people think of government as the work of the legislative branch or the executive branch. This is too simplistic. An analogy that we find useful can be made with the process of industrial selling. In selling to industry, it is never assumed that one individual is the only person who makes a buying decision. As Webster and Wind (1972) point out, this process includes users, influencers, buyers, deciders and gatekeepers. While the interests of all these people need to be taken into account before a sale can be made, often different people are likely to exercise more power in different situations. Likewise, in the political decision-making process, it is important to understand the system deeply enough so that you know not only who the actors are but what roles they play.

Political systems and the role of the state

Two variables of importance to international enterprise are: the philosophy of the government concerning its role, and the degree of participation of the population in the government.

The first of these dimensions is the degree to which the government believes that it should direct the lives of its inhabitants. On the one hand, some governments may feel that their central purpose is to be actively involved in most aspects of the life of the population. This set of values tends to lead to centralized systems of decision making in the country. On the other hand, some governments take the view that limited government intervention in the economy is necessary for the well-being of the country's population. Carried to its extreme, this philosophy suggests that the basic (and possibly only) role of government is to maintain order, supply limited infrastructure (roads, sanitary services and the like) and provide for the defence of the nation in question.

The second dimension is the degree of participation in government. Again, in the extreme, this suggests that a country could adopt procedures that involve most of its citizens in the direct day-to-day governance of the society, while others would involve only a few. Generally speaking, those governments which have a relatively high level of participation are called 'democracies', and those with a relatively low level of participation are called 'totalitarian'. It is obvious that these two poles are not represented by real governments in today's political environment. The point we are making is that these are poles on a continuum and that different countries are closer or further away from these poles. Figure 3 suggests how some governments might fall on a grid of these two variables.

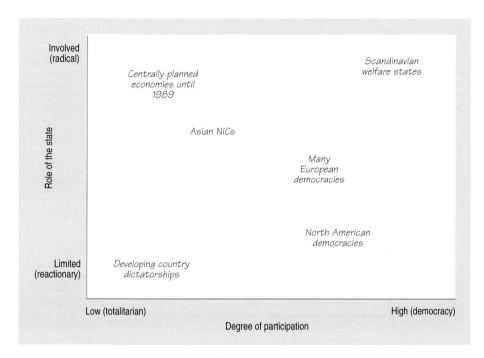

Figure 3   Governments can be seen to vary in two dimensions

The point of this figure is not to describe exactly where on the grid a government may lie. Rather, it suggests that countries that are similar in either of the two dimensions will have similar political systems, and those that are less similar will have fundamentally different political systems. Let us look in more depth at the dimensions.

Participation

In general, countries in which people share the political power, and all that goes with it, with their rulers will face fewer of the tensions within society that come from the loss of voice in governance. A people's need for voice in their governance is like a rubber band. When allowed freedom, the simple exercise of voice leads to low tension levels. The rubber band is relaxed. In regimes where voice is not allowed, a degree of tension arises, and the metaphorical rubber band stretches. Too much tension, and the rubber band breaks. Sudden release of tension, and the rubber band snaps back with force. For this reason, sudden political upheavals such as *coups d'état* and revolutions may occur.

In the past, some people have been tempted to equate capitalism with democracy and socialism with authoritarian regimes. This is not, however, an accurate generalization. There are highly centralized and authoritarian regimes that have pursued typically capitalist economic policies. You can look to the East Asian newly industrialized countries (NICs) for examples of this. Only recently have the governments of some of these countries loosened their grip over power and allowed their general public some degree of participation in politics. Likewise, it has been argued that the emerging 'market socialism' of the People's Republic of China will soon show that socialism does not necessarily imply centralization.

The role of the state

The second dimension of importance is the extent to which the state intervenes in trade and business activities. Extreme cases can be found at either end of the continuum, but a great variety exists between. In many developing countries the government plays an all-pervasive and crucial role in the management of the economy as well as in politics.

There are also variations here. India, for long a protectionist centralized economy, has recently opened up its market and allowed some degree of trade liberalization. A few years ago, Mexico and Chile, having suffered from the consequences of their debt crises, adopted a decentralized and liberal economic and trade policy, largely as a condition for receiving loans from the International Monetary Fund (IMF) and the World Bank.

In advanced industrialized countries the picture is patchy too. In the USA and the UK, especially when conservative parties are in power, governments usually adopt a relatively hands-off policy, certainly with regard to the manufacturing sector, compared with their liberal or socialist counterparts. In Japan, France and many NICs, governments play a more active role in the management of the economy. The countries of the former Soviet bloc are currently in the process of moving from centrally planned economies to more decentralized market-oriented ones, with varying degrees of success. In China, signs of decentralization of economic policies can be seen. While there are regions of China that are practically run on a market economy model, the political and economic system of the country as a whole is still highly centralized.

These two dimensions are important to international managers because they can help to analyse the general political climate in a given country. More participation is likely to lead to a greater degree of influence on governmental policy, while less participation may lead to more sudden and tumultuous change. Governments with strongly interventionist policies will need to be assessed and monitored more closely than those with a more *laissez-faire* attitude towards companies.

Managers who are given responsibility for investment decisions will need expert advice on the strength and stability of governments in countries where their company is considering investment. The approach we have suggested here is one way in which different countries can be compared in making that investment decision.

Activity 2

Select three or four different countries across the world you know could be of possible current interest to your company for investment or exporting.

(a) How would you compare them from the standpoint of political stability and state involvement in commercial activities?

(b) How could your company be affected by your answers and how would it take these issues into account when making an investment decision?

Comment _____

You will have probably considered that countries that are politically unstable have a more risky investment climate and that it is always safer to go for countries where there is at least a strong democratic tradition. On the other hand, countries may seem unstable but in reality may not always be so from a business point of view. They may want to buy goods and services and be prepared to pay for them rather than expect long payment terms because they need to do business. There may be capital available, a lack of restrictive controls and strong government links, which can speed up the investment process. While you might not be sure how the investment decision is taken in your company, you can now see why the political situation is a key factor. How different considerations are taken into account in the decision to invest or export to a country is discussed in more detail later in this unit.

1.3   OTHER ORGANIZATIONS

Often when we think of government, we think exclusively in terms of national or local political entities. For example, one might think of the government of the state of New York, the French government, or the government of Singapore. For the international manager this exclusive focus obscures the fact that much of what is important to their jobs is decided not at the national level but rather at the international level. International enterprise operates within a complex web of international governing bodies that (depending on the industry) can seriously influence their ways of doing business. If your major work is in the European Union you will already be aware of the major influence that EU-wide standards and rules have on your organization's actions. But there are other bodies that have major influence on the international activities of a firm. Among them are specialist bodies dealing with the harmonization of standards in a given industry, regional groupings, and global organizations. The sections below provide examples outlining each

The web pages associated with this unit have several links to web sites that detail the work of international bodies. We would encourage you to visit a few of them to gain a fuller understanding of the scope of their activities.

of these. Our discussion here is brief: a detailed consideration of these myriad bodies would fill a manual the size of this course.

Specialist bodies

Every year I tutor this course I find students whose work is intimately involved with the regulation of the industry in which they operate. Some of these involve voluntary agreements between members of an industry, and other groups are sponsored by regional or global bodies; their agreements have the force of law. For example, this year, I have a student in each category. One student is the managing director of a security printing firm that produces airlines tickets, and another sits on a technical committee that is responsible for harmonizing digital television standards across the EU.

In searching the web for information on these two types of specialist body, I found 186 separate web sites of trade associations at the Yahoo search site. These ranged from 'The Air Movement & Control Association International, Inc.' to the 'World Wide Pet Supply Association'. Many of the organizations with a web presence are actively involved in setting voluntary standards, in influencing governmental decisions, and in promoting the interests of their industries at the national and international level. More importantly, managers from firms in each industry are the key actors in the work of the organizations.

In a similar search for United Nations organizations, I found over 100 UN bodies with a web presence. (The UN is but one of the many examples I could have used.) Many of these are bodies such as the Universal Postal Union (UPU), the International Civil Aviation Organization (ICAO), the International Telecommunication Union (ITU) and the International Maritime Organization (IMO). All of these have regulatory influence through international conventions on the activities of key industries. Let us look in a little more detail at the IMO.

The IMO is the UN's specialized agency responsible for improving maritime safety and preventing pollution from ships. Beginning in the 1980s, members of government bodies and representatives of the shipping industry came together to engage in a process that would achieve the goals of the IMO: improving safety and reducing pollution in shipping. The body decided (to quote the organization's web site):

> ... that the best way of achieving this would be through the International Convention for the Safety of Life at Sea, 1974 (SOLAS). This was done by means of amendments adopted on 24 May 1994, which added a new Chapter IX to the Convention entitled 'Management for the safe operation of Ships'. The Code itself is not actually included in the Convention, but is made mandatory by means of a reference in Chapter IX. ... The main purpose of the new chapter is to make the International Safety Management (ISM) Code mandatory. By adding the ISM Code to SOLAS it is intended to provide an international standard for the safe management of ships and for pollution prevention.

> *(The IMO at http://www.imo.org/imo/ismcode/ismcode.htm)*

Regional groupings

There are important regional groupings, such as the European Union (EU), the North American Free Trade Area (NAFTA) and the Association of South-East Asian Nations (ASEAN). Monitoring, analysing and lobbying the EU, for example, may be as important for a country doing business across the European Union as it is to monitor the individual countries of the EU. That is why many large multinational companies have government affairs offices in Brussels.

The role of the European Commission, in particular, which proposes EU legislation, is of considerable significance to companies. It interprets competition policy issues on behalf of Member States and also has to agree to major mergers and acquisitions. In 1998, the Commission played a major role in extricating concessions from the £24 billion MCI/ WorldCom merger because of its concern over the merged company's potential stranglehold on the international Internet market. The $13 billion merger between Boeing and McDonnell was also subject to EU intervention, because of its implications for competition in the EU, even though both companies are American-owned. The British Airways tie-up with American Airlines is still (1998) waiting for clearance, after two years of scrutiny.

Companies need to spend a great deal of effort on this aspect of business–government relations, as the decisions made by the EU can make or break a deal. In Germany, for example, the proposed digital television tie-up between Deutsche Telecom and two other companies was prevented by the Commission, and its scepticism over a £5 billion merger between Reed Elsevier and Wolters meant that this merger was called off.

Regional organizations, therefore, may need to be treated very carefully and work with them may be considerable, especially if they have legal powers of interpretation and enforcement of company law and the right to fine (as does the Commission) companies which break EU regulations. Other institutions, such as the Council of Ministers, the European Parliament and the Court of Justice, may also be involved as part of a company's external relations with the European Union.

Global organizations

Global organizations, such as the United Nations, the Organization for Economic Co-operation and Development (OECD) and the World Trade Organization (WTO) may also be of considerable importance to companies. Progress towards world standards for telecommunications, for example, may be slow, as may an agreement on ethical standards for international business. Nevertheless, the work of global organizations needs to be understood by companies, not just in terms of compliance, but because what companies say about international organizations could have an important effect on their public relations and company image.

Activity 3 _____

The European Union is of growing importance to the countries who are currently members (15 in 1999 and a further 10 likely to join over the next few years). Because so many policies affecting business are proposed and agreed at the EU level, companies need to understand how it functions, monitor its activities and be prepared to contribute to influencing its decisions. If you were the corporate affairs manager responsible for these activities, how would you carry them out and what information would you need? Use your existing knowledge or find other sources of information. Do not look at the comment until you have given the questions some thought yourself.

Comment

There is an abundance of information available. The European weekly newspaper is useful, the European pages of the Economist are helpful and, if you have time to read the two or three pages of European news in the Financial Times, you and your company will be very well informed. The European Commission offices around the world and its web site will provide you with as much information as you want. In particular, 'The week in Europe', available free from the UK Commission Office, is an invaluable weekly checklist (see the references at end of the unit for details). Analysing and converting the wealth of information into useful material for decision makers in your company is a different matter. It will only need to know about the key issues and not too frequently and not at great length. Major issues rumble on for months, if not years, so there is no need to get your colleagues excited too early. You may want to use consultants, or certainly visit Brussels two or three times a year. A large company will have an office in Brussels, but maintaining it is expensive and perhaps using a Brussels-based consultant and visiting, or ensuring that your top managers visit at least once a year, can be a successful way of developing your EU relations. What sort of things should you monitor? Your trade association will have good ideas about this and so will UNICE, which is the Brussels-based federation of the major EU employers' federations, such as the CBI in the UK and the Patronat in France.

You will need to monitor pipeline legislation emanating from the European Commission. You will need to make contact with European Commission officials dealing with policies relevant to your business, such as the Single Market Programme, competition and industrial policies, social affairs, energy, telecommunications and fiscal policies, to name but a few.

You should contact members of the European Parliament, especially those in whose region you operate, and invite them to visit your offices or plant. They can be very helpful with introductions. Your company may want to appoint a non-executive director who has had broad experience of EU operations, perhaps as a diplomat in Brussels or as the manager of a multinational company operating in several EU countries.

You can learn more about the ways in which the EU impinges on your business by reading 'How the European Union works and how it affects business' in the Supplemental Readings.

1.4 THE BALANCE OF POWER BETWEEN COMPANIES AND GOVERNMENTS

We suggested earlier that the relationship between a company and a government is not a one-way process with the government laying down the conditions under which companies must function. The relationship is rather one of mutual power and influence.

There are roughly 200 countries in the world in which a company can conceivably operate. Each of these represents a possible source of markets, production locations or supplies. While it is possible that a company could do all three activities (market, produce and purchase) in every country of the world, this is not likely. Likewise, there is a myriad of firms in the world. Each one of these firms could make available to host countries a degree of managerial or technical expertise, capital, jobs and the like.

The ability of both countries and companies to make choices from this multitude of actors leads to the observation that countries and companies both have a degree of power in their relationships with each other. In short, if a country will not give a company what it wants, there are other countries it can choose. Likewise, if a company will not give a country what it wants, another one probably will.

This notion of relative degrees of power between players on the international stage leads to what could be called 'the golden rule' of bargaining power. This is shown in Figure 4.

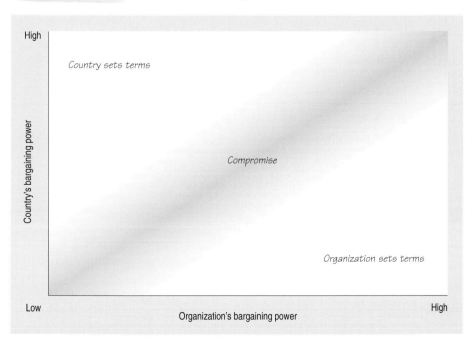

Figure 4   The golden rule of bargaining power

When the government of a given country has a high relative level of bargaining power, it will be in a position to dictate terms to any organization wanting to operate within its borders. Obviously, when an organization has a high level of this power, the opposite will be the case. When relative levels of power are the same, some accommodation between the two parties is likely to occur.

What factors increase the bargaining power of the actors? Broadly speaking, anything one party wants, and the other party has, is eligible for consideration. This bald statement clearly needs to be modified by the availability of the 'want' from other sources. In that sense, the relationship between governments and firms is like a market-place. Table 1 suggests a few of the forces that impinge upon the bargaining power of nations and of companies.

Table 1 Forces that affect the bargaining power of countries and companies	
Countries	**Companies**
• The size of the country: economic, demographic and geographic	• The size of the company: economic strength and geographic spread
• The technological infrastructure available in the country	• The distinctive technological competence of the company available for transfer to the host country
• The skills of the country's workforce	• The managerial competence of the company
• The nature and levels of inducements and restrictions to trade	• The number and influence of local allies available to the company
• The desirability of the market	• The adaptability of the company to local conditions
• The availability of necessary supplies	• The reputation of the company (with other countries)
• The number of feasible alternative countries	• The number of feasible alternative companies
• The solidarity of this country with others on a given set of issues (i.e. its membership of regional or global organizations)	• The solidarity of this company with others on a given set of issues (i.e. its membership of trade associations)
• The political stability of the country	• The level of home country support
• Other specific attributes of the company	• Other specific attributes of the company

Countries seem to want: revenue; secure jobs for their populations; economic and industrial development; balance of payments adjustments; health, safety and environmental protection; and technology transfer. They may also have agendas that include political goals and national security goals as part of their 'wants'.

Companies, on the other hand, seem to desire (in addition to the all-encompassing word 'profit'): resources (supplies, labour and infrastructure); stability; managerial control; flexibility; and fairness in terms of regulation, taxation and incentives.

In the early stages of the 'courtship' process between country and company, these issues are often clear and articulate. As relationships grow and change, they may become obscure and disagreement and conflict may arise.

Conflicts within any set of parties can centre on goals, roles, procedures, and behaviours that are at variance with each other. The usual sorts of issue over which countries and companies come into conflict are suggested in Section 2.

Activity 4

Consider one of the host countries in which your company operates. Using the ideas presented in Section 1.4, describe the sources of power of your own company in that country.

Comment

The example we have chosen is the work of the Open University Business School in Hungary. We shall use the categories in Table 1 for the Comment.

Table 2 Sources of power for the OUBS in Hungary	
Category	**Our source of power**
The size of the company: economic strength and geographic spread	We have more European students than any other business school. This experience and spread gives us an advantage over multinational companies operating in many nations.
The distinctive technological competence of the company available for transfer to the host	No organization has more experience in distance teaching than we have. We are willing and able to transfer our technology to a host country partner with no omissions.
The managerial competence of the company	We are willing to devote managerial time to our activities in the country. In addition, we are willing to support and train our partners to increase their managerial competence.

The number and influence of local allies available to the company	We have supporters currently well placed in the government.
The adaptability of the company to local conditions	We are willing to work with the host country to translate our (non-MBA) material. On the down side, we can modify our systems only slightly to take account of local conditions.
The reputation of the company (with other countries)	Our partners in some countries are units of government. We believe our relationships are sound, in which case so is our reputation.
The number of feasible alternative companies	There are several other companies wanting to do what we do in Hungary. This therefore reduces our power.
The level of home country support	The British Council and the UK government give us effective support.

1.5 CONCLUSION

Our main argument in this section has been that the notion of stakeholder is important in determining the sources of opportunity and threat to firms. We suggested also that you need to understand the national and international stakeholders in your company.

We have argued that governments are major stakeholders of organizations. Governments are similar in that each of them has certain functions that they must accomplish. While these functions are similar, countries differ in the ways in which they organize themselves, and the task of the manager is to understand at least the broad outlines of how these functions are organized in each country in which they have dealings. The specialist manager working, perhaps, in the corporate affairs function, will need access to comprehensive information about the role and functions of government in the host country.

We have also suggested that political systems vary in dimensions of ideology and have developed two dimensions that are important to firms. These are the level of participation of the population in governance, and the government's philosophy about its role in society.

We reminded you that the relationships between a company and individual host governments are not the only concern for managers: other actors with supranational influences are also important. We listed a few of these actors and suggested that, if you come into contact with them, you should learn more about their structures and functions.

Finally, we looked at the balance of power between governments and companies. The relationship is not one-sided: both parties have influence based upon what they want and what they can offer the other party. When this influence is in balance, compromise occurs. When it is out of balance, one party sets the terms of the bargains that are struck.

In the next section, we turn to the question 'What types of opportunities and threats arise for firms as they operate across borders?'

2 RELATIONSHIPS: THE SOURCE OF POLITICAL ISSUES

2.1 BUSINESS–GOVERNMENT RELATIONSHIPS

Home government relationships

Governments are interested in what companies based in their countries do at home and abroad because of the economic, political and cultural implications of their activities. For these reasons, the government of the country of the parent company usually exerts a fair amount of control. There can be at least three sources of such control:

- the home country's legal jurisdiction over the firm
- formal and informal ties between senior managers of the organization and government top officials
- the concentration of the firm's assets in its home base.

Companies are usually based in the country in which they are legally incorporated. When this is the case, the home government has the ability to compel certain actions affecting the entire company. The home country can, for instance, alter financial flows, change trade patterns, alter competition rules, control the flow of technology, alter patterns of inter-firm pricing and restrict the movement of people.

Top managers of the companies and senior government ministers and officials are often members of the same socio-cultural strata. Sometimes ex-ministers are engaged as senior directors in these firms or successful industrialists are given senior positions in the government. This interchangeability serves to influence the policies of both parties.

Home country governments can also be great allies of their home country firms. They may exert pressure on host governments where the interests of their companies are concerned. For instance, as Daniels and Radebaugh (1989) argue, governments have in the past used the promise of aid or the threat to withhold it as a means of extracting from host governments terms that are more acceptable to their investors. For example, the UK government obtained an opt-out clause for UK companies on the Social Chapter of EU legislation. This responded to the wishes of much of UK business, which felt the conditions were too onerous and made for higher than desirable labour costs. In 1997, however, the new labour government reversed the decision.

Host government relationships

While equal treatment of host and home country companies is a principle enshrined in international law, it somehow seems that there are often ways of requiring foreign firms to work to different standards. Host governments may take various actions against foreign companies for political or economic reasons. These actions range from interfering in the foreign organization's managerial policies, harassment and making it difficult to carry out its operations, to outright nationalization and confiscation of the organization's assets. (Note that the most severe actions mentioned in this paragraph are very rarely taken. The relationships between increasingly sophisticated companies and governments have improved substantially over time. Thus governmental action such as nationalization is best seen as a relic of the past.)

Foreign firms may be required to include local nationals in their top management teams, and to use a certain proportion of local components in the assembly of products from largely imported components. Companies may offer (as part of their government relations programme), or be asked, to build or contribute to the construction of local amenities such as roads, houses for employees, hospitals, schools and similar facilities in the areas where they are located. Governments may (rarely) also take actions that are primarily aimed at driving a foreign firm out of their country. The actions include encouraging the organization's employees to strike and asking consumers to boycott its products, as was the outcome of the friction between Malaysia and the UK in 1994.

Governments may require foreign firms to pay excessive licence fees and high taxes. Such charges can be increased to the point where making profits is not possible and the firms are forced to leave. Firms may not be allowed to take out their profits and/or may be forced to invest them in specific governmental projects. These acts are often referred to as 'creeping expropriation'.

There can be many reasons behind a government's actions against foreign firms operating in its territories. The most significant types of action and their underlying reasons are discussed below.

A change in or a shift of emphasis in foreign trade policies

An example of this is the decision of the Indian government in the late 1970s to change, on protectionist grounds, the conditions under which foreign companies could invest and operate in India. This made it very difficult, if not impossible, for companies like Coca-Cola to continue their presence in the country. A recent change of policy shifted the emphasis towards attracting foreign investment and, as a result, Coca-Cola, among others, is back. India, like China, has had different policies towards foreign companies and inward investment. The current and future political climate in both countries needs regular monitoring by companies doing business there.

A change of the government itself

Governmental change, whether through constitutional or other means, can lead to difficulties for companies if the change of government brings into power a party that wants to change its policies towards foreign companies.

Democratic elections, although they are not dramatic methods of changing a government, can nevertheless have serious consequences for foreign firms. While the current global trend is for privatization, some commentators suggest that, should conditions change substantially, many countries around the world may begin to renationalize their industries.

Coups d'états are often viewed by foreign firms as a great risk, although this is probably not justified. In less democratic societies, such as some Latin American, African and Asian countries, a *coup d'état* was, and may still be, the only means by which people could change their governments. The coups are usually a way of settling domestic power struggles and scoring points among rivals, and the new governments often follow similar foreign trade policies to their predecessors.

Revolutions, such as those in Iran and Nicaragua in the late 1970s, had serious consequences for foreign firms located in those countries and for the trade between them and the Western world. In both countries, the new governments took a hard anti-US line in their foreign policies. As a result, the assets of many US and other Western firms were confiscated without compensation. This in turn provoked the USA and its allies to impose on Iran and Nicaragua an embargo on trade and investment and a freezing of Iran's funds held in US banks.

Trade and tariff issues

Governments may use foreign trade and tariff rules to regulate trade and investment flows.

Tariffs. Tariffs are taxes that a government levies on goods imported into the country. They are not only a means of import control and protection but also a source of revenue for governments. The level of a tariff is usually related to the value of the goods. The aim is to make the traded goods dearer for the end-customers and hence discourage their trade. High tariffs on foreign imports are often levied on 'infant industries' in order to provide protection to domestic producers during the early start-up years of an industry's existence.

Domestic content. Many companies include a certain quantity of locally made components in the production of goods in their subsidiaries. Some governments take this element of local content into consideration when defining the origins of the products. On the basis of this definition, they then decide whether to subject the products to tariffs or other import barriers.

The French government's attitude to Japanese manufactured goods, especially cars, was a good example in this connection. Before EU intervention, the government imposed an import quota on Japanese cars, and extended the coverage of this quota to cars made by Japanese firms in other countries. The French government defines such cars as Japanese unless at least 80 per cent of their components are made in the host countries.

Rules, regulations and procedures

Some governments have liberal rules on foreign direct investment within their territory. In these cases, a foreign firm may own up to 100 per cent of a locally based company. Some governments allow only joint ventures, with varying degrees of permitted ownership by foreign investors. A majority shareholding does have an advantage for a foreign company, but it may not be necessary because host countries need to attract foreign investment and will not, therefore, want to upset foreign companies. Governments, of course, always have the final say, because they can change the laws!

Governments may introduce regulations governing the contents of imported goods, ostensibly for reasons such as health and safety, the environment and technical standards, and this would effectively reduce imports.

Standard procedures can also be used to discourage foreign exporters. For instance, French customs officials insisted that Poitiers (an inland town) would be the port of entry for Japanese video recorders. When these came into the country, every single unit was inspected in detail, thereby lengthening the waiting and queuing time for trucks and lorries carrying these goods from ports to French customs. The usual procedure for the goods imported from other countries was random checking.

Most countries, when purchasing goods and services, favour their home companies to some extent. Some countries' rules and regulations require the governments to give special preferences to domestic suppliers over those from abroad, even though the latter might be able to offer better and cheaper deals. A more recent non-tariff barrier to trade occurred when French turkeys were banned from being imported into the UK because of the fear of Newcastle disease, a disease which seemed to occur around Christmas, thus inadvertently (or not) preventing the import of French turkeys to compete with home-produced ones at the time of seasonal high consumption of turkey meat.

Taxation

While the question of taxation is covered in detail in the Finance unit in the second part of the course, it is important to note here that multinational companies come under the jurisdiction of more than one tax authority. Since each country has its own taxation rules and regulations, a multinational company is subjected to various taxation treatments concurrently.

Moreover, countries differ in their position towards foreign companies. Some would like to encourage inward foreign direct investment, and use tax incentives to this end; some use high taxes in order to discourage the repatriation of foreign companies' profits.

Countries also differ in the way they tax home country firms operating abroad. Under US tax law, for instance, the income of a foreign branch of a US parent company is treated differently from the income of foreign subsidiaries. A foreign branch is legally regarded as an integral extension of the parent, and its profits are automatically included in those of the parent company. These are taxed by the US government for the period in which they are earned. A subsidiary is viewed as a separate legal entity, and its profits are not generally taxable by the USA until they are repatriated to the parent firm as dividends (Weekly and Aggarwal, 1987).

The differences in taxation laws and rules between various countries have of course significant implications for companies. For instance, companies might find countries with a low rate of tax and favourable incentives more attractive as the site for their production plants than high-tax countries.

Also, tax laws can influence companies' decisions about the type of affiliates they want to set up abroad. As Weekly and Aggarwal point out, given the US tax laws referred to above, a US company might, for example, decide to set up a branch rather than a subsidiary abroad, and include the operational losses of the early years in the overall profit and loss account of the company as a whole. This would reduce the company's taxable profits.

While there are legal prohibitions against its abuse in most countries, transfer pricing is another practice that has been used to make the most of tax differentials between countries. Companies buy from or sell to their own subsidiaries and other affiliates across national boundaries. The price at which these transactions take place, the transfer price, might be recorded at a high level if the subsidiary concerned is located in a high-tax country. In this way, the subsidiary shows a much reduced profit or even losses. Transfer pricing may also be used to repatriate funds from a high-tax country, ostensibly as a price paid for goods and services bought from a subsidiary in another country.

Multinational companies create non-operating subsidiaries or branches in 'tax haven' countries in order to reduce or defer tax payments. Tax havens are typically very small nations with limited resources of their own, which deliberately keep their taxes low in order to encourage multinational companies to set up affiliated offices there. Barbados, the Bahamas and Liechtenstein are examples.

While companies may have taken advantage of lax regulations in the past, it should be emphasized that companies rarely become involved in illegal transactions as regards transfer pricing. The continuing struggle between national authorities and companies is conducted within the context of a legal framework with the objective of both sides to negotiate the optimum deal for themselves. The result is inevitably one of compromise.

A major issue concerning the taxation of companies is international double taxation. When this occurs, profit is subjected to tax under the systems of two or more countries. Countries usually agree, through multilateral and bilateral treaties (for example, the OECD's Convention for the Avoidance of Double Taxation) to prevent multinational companies from being double-taxed, but there is considerable scope for interpretation of complex rules on both sides.

Mergers and acquisitions and competition policy

As you will see in the Strategy unit in the second part of the course, many multinationals find it advantageous to buy a competitor in a host country as a way of gaining access to markets, to supplies, to technology or to product lines. Two sets of government policies have an influence on these companies.

First, as we have seen above, many governments have policies on the ownership of their countries' corporate entities. Some countries have clear policies that affect the ease of mergers and acquisitions. The regulations in place in a given country will make it easier or more difficult for a foreign company to buy a host country company. In 1994, Switzerland and Germany were criticized (possibly unfairly) in the press for making the purchase of their national firms too difficult.

The second type of policy is competition policy (or, as it is called in the USA, anti-trust legislation). Competition policy is designed to limit the concentration of economic power and to promote optimum conditions for competition in the country. Companies whose business gives them high market share in a given country (or in the case of the EU, the region) are prohibited from acquiring competitors if the acquisition would 'distort' competition.

Legal practices

Not only do governments have different competition regulations but also they have different legal systems. Laws are often based on English 'common law'. This system places great emphasis on normal 'custom and practices' to establish the principles upon which disputes will be resolved. This is not to say that governments that use common law do not have a legislative function but that history also has a role to play. In other parts of the world, laws are based on the idea that one can legislate for anything. These systems use 'code-based law'. Much of Europe has gained its legal framework from the 'code Napoleon', which itself was based on earlier codes of the late Roman and Byzantine periods. A special Islamic code-based law is practised in some Middle Eastern and Asian countries where laws are derived from religious writings.

Some countries regulate the day-to-day business operations of companies closely; some control only those larger-scale movements and operations of a foreign enterprise that could have a direct effect on the domestic economy.

The Canadian government, for instance, reserves the right to regulate certain aspects of the operations of international companies, such as when an existing foreign-controlled organization wants to diversify into new and unrelated industries within Canada. The expansion of already established companies into 'related' business is, however, left unhindered (Wallace, 1982).

The governments of most industrialized countries tend to exert rather less control over the *operational* activities of multinational companies (for example, their initial capital inflows, local borrowing, inter-corporate debt, transfer pricing, capital transfers among affiliates, and profit allocations). The reason may be that these countries not only host the majority of multinationals but also are home to many of them. Therefore, unreasonable actions and unnecessary interference with the legal business operations of their guest companies might provoke retaliation by fellow industrialized countries that host theirs (Wallace, 1982).

Under international law, all firms should be subject to 'national treatment'. This means that host countries treat foreign-controlled enterprises under their own laws, regulations and administrative practices in a manner consistent with international law, and no less favourably than they treat domestic enterprises in comparable situations (OECD, 1976). Although most nations subscribe to the 'national treatment' principle on paper, in practice they do not always fully adhere to it. A difficulty that is often the cause for dispute is the requirement for an agreement to be interpreted according to the laws of a particular country. To avoid conflict, companies will often agree to have disputes negotiated according to the laws of a third country, such as Switzerland, which is considered a reasonable compromise, although most countries still prefer to be under the jurisdiction of their own home country, if possible.

Codes of conduct

The question of the relationship between companies and host governments has been the topic of heated debate over the past 40 years, and the issues being debated have tended to be framed in ethical terms. The controversy is partially due to the sometimes disproportionate economic power exercised by large companies in their relationships with smaller, less economically developed countries. It is also true that, historically, some companies have not always been 'good citizens' of their host countries. Large, economically powerful companies have caused environmental damage (for example, the Union Carbide release of toxic chemicals in Bhopal), bribed governmental officials (many military hardware suppliers), and even (successfully) attempted to overthrow legitimately elected governments (the Allende government in Chile).

The criticisms have resulted in calls by governments and international organizations to strengthen systems for resolving international disputes and codes of conduct that should be adhered to by all organizations operating across borders. Several of these codes exist, proposed by the UN and other international bodies. For example, the OECD has issued guidelines for multinational enterprises (MNEs) and labour relations, which have the objective of improving 'the foreign investment climate by encouraging positive contribution to economic and social progress that MNEs can make while minimizing the difficulties arising from their operations.' The guidelines impose duties on MNEs to disclose financial and operating information, meet standards of labour relations, avoid competition-limiting activities, consider national balance of payments objectives in their financial dealings, and co-operate in technology transfer (Rugman *et al.*, 1985).

The monitoring and regulation of the international business regime has improved significantly over recent decades and both business and government have come to understand their interdependence. As a result, greater fairness and responsibility are exhibited by both sides. The relations of business and government will never be separated and there will always be tensions. The aim, on both sides, is to make these tensions as creative and beneficial as possible.

Activity 5

In 1997, the UK launched an ethics policy for dealing with arms sales to foreign countries. If you were to develop an ethics policy for your company, what points would you include in it and how would you enforce it?

Comment

The issue of ethics in business is of growing concern to many stakeholders in our increasingly global society. Professors of ethics are being appointed in business schools and organizations such as the OECD have drawn up ethical guidelines for companies. Several companies subscribe to these guidelines and most large companies have an explicit, as well as an implicit, ethics policy.

It is not an easy area, because what is considered normal in one country may well be illegal in another. 'Introduction fees' are demanded by well-connected people in some countries to ensure that business happens at all. Governments may require underhand payments and winners of official national tenders may only be those companies that have paid off, in one way or another, those involved in the tendering process.

Some highly ethical companies refuse to do business if there is any hint of the need to bribe, but such activities range along a continuum and it is very difficult to draw the line. State visits by leaders of countries are often occasions to make important business deals and are considered legitimate. Countries offer tax incentives to companies who invest. Agents are paid commission on the completion of successful business deals.

Major companies are clear that they cannot be involved in bribery and usually say so. They have to monitor what their employees are doing on their behalf and this may not always be easy. Legal penalties for directors involved in bribery in many countries make it inadvisable and illegal to indulge in the practice, but is it immoral to do so when that is the only way of doing business in some countries? Even governments of reputable countries may indulge in, or condone, industrial espionage and feed information on possible foreign contracts to interested firms.

These issues will not go away and companies and individuals need increasingly to be sure of their views and ensure that governments of the countries in which they operate are aware of them.

This is a suitable point at which to review the Ethics audio cassette and the associated case studies in the Media Notes.

2.2 RELATIONSHIPS BETWEEN GOVERNMENTS

As we have already said, nations engage in political, economic, cultural and other types of relationship in pursuance of their interests. The kind and quality of the relationships between nations have an effect on the organizations operating within them. Moreover, the nature of these relationships usually changes over time. A change of relationships between governments caused by political reforms (as in Eastern Europe) or by war (as in the Gulf War) could change the political climate within which foreign firms and international trade operate. In the case of the reforms in East European countries, for instance, the change led to co-operation and friendship between these countries and most of the rest of the world. In contrast, the conflict and animosity between the two sides in the Gulf War posed threats and instability that diverted the attention, energy and resources of many organizations from their main activities in the region.

Wars, especially when they are over, can also offer fertile ground for opportunities that may not have existed before. The Gulf War is a good case in point. The reconstruction of Kuwait's infrastructure and the capping of its burning oil wells, and the demand by Middle-Eastern countries for intelligent missiles and smart bombs such as those used by the Allied forces, were among the new opportunities that were created in the region by the war.

Governments can still cause problems for companies even if they are not officially at war with one another. They may, for instance, restrict exports to countries that are perceived as politically hostile. For example, Western countries used to ban exports of high-technology industrial and consumer goods to the Soviet bloc before the end of the Cold War. The main objective here was to stop the communists from using Western technology to military advantage.

Governments may also restrict or boycott imports from certain countries as a form of punishment. Examples are the US boycott of imports of coffee from Nicaragua under the Sandanistas regime, and trade sanctions against South Africa, which were seen by most nations as a means of bringing about the abolition of the apartheid regime in that country.

The reverse is also true. Some powerful industrialized countries export to developing countries at a much lower price than world prices in order to influence them politically and otherwise. Governments also co-operate with one another through global, regional and bilateral agreements to facilitate, among other things, the operations of their international companies and to protect the interests of their citizens.

2.3 CONCLUSION

We have seen in this section that a feature of the political scene is business–government relationships. We have shown you that home countries impinge upon the activities of their companies in a variety of ways. We have also shown you some of the ways in which host countries affect foreign companies. This can result from a change of government or the political climate in a country. Countries can use trade and tariff restrictions, fiscal policy and competition laws to influence company behaviour. All of these take place within a wide variety of legal systems that you will have to become familiar with as your job requires you to operate across the world.

In the next section, we look at the ways in which companies can deal with the threats and opportunities generated by these relationship issues.

3 STRATEGIES FOR ASSESSING THE EXTERNAL ENVIRONMENT

So far, the emphasis of this unit has been on understanding the political issues organizations are likely to face when they cross borders. These issues are similar to those faced by organizations operating only in a domestic environment but they are made more complex by the diversity of political systems in the world. As pointed out in Section 2, however, companies need not simply accept whatever comes their way from the political environment. Broadly speaking, there are three strategies that companies use to manage their political environment.

1 Understand it. Two techniques are available for this: the first relates to the entry decisions made by companies and is called, somewhat pessimistically, 'political risk assessment'; the second, which is used by several companies, is called 'issue monitoring'.

2 Buffer their activities against stakeholder action.

3 Influence stakeholder actions that might impinge upon their operations. There are a variety of processes used for this, including lobbying and public relations activities.

3.1 UNDERSTAND: FRAMEWORKS FOR GENERATING INFORMATION

Understanding of the political scene is essential only to the extent that companies are likely to be affected by governmental actions. The ways in which politics impinges upon companies differ depending on whether the company is currently operating in a country. It is therefore important to distinguish between techniques used before a company enters a new country and those used after it has begun its operations there. The process used before entry is usually called *political risk analysis*. The process used when a company has the requisite local resources is called *issue monitoring*.

Assessing political risk

Political risk assessment systems are used to decide the level of risk inherent in entering a new country. If a country is too 'risky', a company will probably choose to avoid it in favour of another less risky or more profitable one. The decision to move to one country or another is too often made with little or no analysis. The logic of 'opportunity cost' suggests that this is unwise.

We define opportunity cost as the amount (of strategic benefit or money) lost by not using a resource in the best possible way. Opportunity cost is thus associated with choosing one option over another. When (as is usually the case) resources are limited, firms need to analyse the options available to them for the use of those resources. The goal of this analysis is to decide which option will be most likely to maximize the attainment of the company's strategic objectives.

If a company decides to move outside its borders, it gives up other options. The gap between the best option and the option taken is the opportunity cost. This is illustrated in Figure 5.

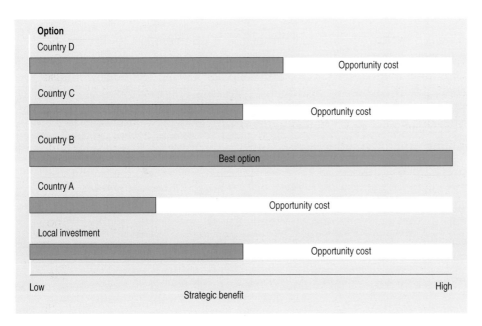

Figure 5   Opportunity cost

A sound decision-making process, which considers all relevant information and results in the best decision possible, is thus necessary. Political risk assessment systems are designed to improve this decision-making process and reduce the opportunity cost associated with less optimum decisions.

All political risk assessment techniques have in common the fact that the company using them cannot use local managers' knowledge and skills if they have no such employees. Firms make use of a variety of different techniques for this process. A few of them are outlined below.

Quantitative methods. These methods use advanced statistical and computer modelling techniques to forecast political risk. In these models, certain variables that are thought to be causally related to drastic political change are used to predict discontinuous political change. However, most of these statistical and computer models fall short of predicting company-specific (micro) future events in their larger forecasts about country-specific (macro) changes. Country-wide political instability does not necessarily mean that there is a great danger of nationalization for a foreign company.

Grand tours. As its name suggests, this technique uses senior managers who travel to a potential host country on a fact-finding mission. There, they collect information on various relevant socio-political factors and make an estimate of the country's political stability. The obvious shortcoming of this method is the superficiality of the information collected.

Old hands. These procedures involve seeking advice from other firms that are currently dealing or have in the past dealt with the targeted country. Consultants currently working in a country can give a great deal of relevant advice to the new entrant. Embassies, trade missions and chambers of commerce are often good and continuing sources of advice.

Delphi method. A variation on the theme of 'old hands', this method involves gathering together a group of 'experts' on the global, regional and specific-country political scenes. Often these experts are professors of politics, former cabinet ministers and the like who are expected to be up to date in the areas of their expertise. The group then holds a seminar attended by the employing organization's management to discuss the political issues in a given country or region. The effectiveness of this method is limited to the quality of the experts and their knowledge of the company involved.

Checklists. These involve ranking a set of countries against a list of potential political hazards, such as governmental stability, administrative competence, domestic tension, official attitudes towards foreign investment, prospects for nationalization, and so on. This method has the advantage of comparing a variety of countries at the same time. The success of the method depends on the accuracy and reliability of the information on which the ranking is based, and on the quality of the judgement of the people using the method.

As noted, each of these methods has a variety of inherent difficulties. In some cases, the method can look at only one nation at a time as a potential candidate for expansion. In others, the quality of the data is critical to the outcome of the decision-making process. In yet others, the skills of the analysts or experts are crucial.

The use of political risk systems

It is important to bear in mind that political risk should be evaluated at the country, industry and organization levels. Also, because of the complexities of modern politics, it is not often easy or possible to forecast political risk. The revolution in Iran in 1979, which led to the overthrow of the pro-USA regime of the Shah, was not detected as a probability by many foreign companies that were operating in the country at the time. This was in spite of all the signs of people's dissatisfaction with the outgoing regime. Neither was the Iraqi invasion of Kuwait on 2 August 1990 considered likely by many people, including many eminent politicians the world over, until it actually happened. In connection with a *coup d'état* in Thailand, *Time* pointed out that:

> ... for weeks there had been confident predictions in Bangkok that a military coup was unlikely, despite obviously escalating tensions between the army and the elected government of [the] Prime Minister. The men in uniform, political analysts contended, would be unwilling to do anything that [might] disrupt a three-year economic boom. That seemed a reasonable judgement – until the tanks began to roll.

> (Time, *4 March 1991, p. 50)*

The fall of the communist regimes in Central and Eastern Europe, the break-up of the former Yugoslavia and the 1997–8 crisis in East Asia similarly were not forecast, which shows the limitations of the process. On the other hand, the steady development of the EU has been carefully monitored and the process has helped shape investment decisions.

A synthesis

As noted above, there are difficulties associated with each of the methods of political risk assessment. We would argue that some variation on the process described in the rest of this section seems to work well for most firms. The system suggested has the virtue that it is relatively low cost, can be conducted by the company's own personnel, and results in easily understandable outcomes. Its major disadvantage is that, as with most systems, the quality of the data used in the system and the skill of the analysts using it are critical.

You should note that the model described is not limited to political issues, and involves all external issues affecting a company.

The process works best when a small group of people work through steps 1 and 2 alone, divide the data-gathering tasks of step 3 among themselves, and discuss the analysis together. The people in the group need to be senior enough in the company to understand the key dynamics of their industry and the company's competitive position within it. Step 4 is best led by a project manager who has an agreed budget to accomplish the task.

Step 1: Start with a list of all the countries in the world

After having decided that further investment of resources in the current activities of the company is clearly not the best alternative, you need to decide which of the world's 200-plus countries is the best for entry. Even if your strategy requires entry into a specific region, it is a good idea to start with all the nations of the world or of the region in which you are interested as potential candidates. You will screen this list in the next steps to eliminate the least appropriate countries.

Step 2: Use common sense

Using the company's strategic reasons for moving into a new country, remove any countries from your list that are clearly not compatible with the strategy. Another way of thinking about this is to use your educated common sense. If, for example, your company is one that produces alcoholic beverages, eliminate those countries which have high populations of Muslims or which for other reasons have banned the sale of your products. Likewise, if a key factor for success in your industry is the availability of a highly literate population, eliminate all countries with high illiteracy rates. Your aim in this step should be to eliminate as many countries as possible without detailed analysis (which takes time and money to do).

Step 3: Screen in detail

Using the reduced list of countries, your goal is to narrow the field further. The strategy at this stage is to work from the broad issues that influence all firms to the narrow issues that have an effect on only your industry and company. You can think of this step as containing three screens, each of which requires data gathering and analysis.

We suggest some of the topics for this analysis on pages 37–39. Note that the first screen is used to check for factors that would preclude your company from entering a given country. This might include information on whether boycotts or sanctions are in place against the country, whether the country has unacceptable local participation or content laws or state monopolies in your industry. General reading and computer searches around each country (you may use the course team's web pages as a starting point) should allow you to do a good job of eliminating more countries from your list. If it is still long, it might be an idea for your group to assign specific countries or topics to different group members at this point.

The second screen requires your group not only to find data but also to judge the importance of the information for your company. Thus, you should note from the screening tool that item weighting is included in the work of the group. Weights are determined by group consensus on a scale of 1 to 10. Thus, if size of GNP and rate of growth (item 1) are thought by your group to be twice as important as trade balance (item 4), and tax rates (item 41) are the most important issue for your company, you might give item 1 a weight of 4, item 4 a weight of 2, and item 41 a weight of 10. Scoring for each country is simply the rank order of the countries based on the data. Where the information you acquire is qualitative, this will again require judgement by the group as to where to rank each country. In order to reduce your workload, it might be a good idea to include for analysis only those data items that are in the top third or half of the weighting scale, eliminating items that are less important to your company.

The third and final screen asks the group to decide what other company- and industry-specific information they might need. For example, if the Open University Business School were thinking about expanding into a new country, we might want to know the number and size of management education courses in that country, the number of English-speaking people, the number of managers in the workforce, and the number of expatriate British managers.

When analysing your data, you will probably note that collecting data on the countries of the world is fraught with difficulty. Data are, in many cases, not comparable from one country to the next. If comparability were the only problem, it would not be too great a difficulty. What is more difficult is that, for many countries, data are not available. Your group will have to decide what to do about missing information when this is the case.

When the data are finally collected, the group will need to meet again to discuss the findings, and to draw up a short-list of between three and five countries for further study. This should be a relatively easy task based on the numerical scores produced by the system.

Screen 1   Eliminating factors

Unacceptable product: standards, safety, socio-cultural factors, etc.

Political barriers: boycotts, sanctions, local participation, state monopolies, etc.

Economic barriers: non-transferability of funds, barter trading, price control, etc.

Legal barriers: anti-trust legislation, labour laws, patents, environmental control, etc.

Supply barriers: shortage of factors of production or infrastructure, etc.

Screen 2   General influencing factors

Factor	Item	Item weight	Country A		Country B			Country N	
			Score	Total	Score	Total		Score	Total
Economic factors	1 Size of GNP and rate of growth								
	2 Nature of development plans								
	3 Resistance to recession								
	4 Trade balance								
	5 Foreign exchange methods								
	6 Stability of currency								
	7 Remittance and repatriation rules								
	8 Balance of economy (industry, agriculture and trade)								
	9 Market for product: size								
	10 Per capita income								
	11 Income distribution								
	12 Inflation rate								
	13 Other								
	Total this section								
Political factors	14 Stability of government								
	15 Conflict between social groups								
	16 Attitude towards private foreign investment (government and other)								
	17 Nationalization threats								
	18 State industry (presence)								
	19 Protectionism								
	20 Political groups: their power								
	21 Other								
	Total this section								
Governmental factors	22 Fiscal and monetary policies								
	23 Competence of bureaucracy								
	24 Fairness of courts								
	25 Modern corporate law structure								
	26 Intellectual property law								
	27 Price controls								
	28 Ownership controls								
	Total this section								

Factor	Item	Item weight	Country A		Country B			Country N	
			Score	Total	Score	Total		Score	Total
Geographical factors	29 Necessary infrastructure (ports, power, roads, communications)								
	30 Raw materials availability								
	31 Distance to markets and suppliers								
	32 Supporting industry (packaging, etc.)								
	33 Ease of import and export								
	34 Cost of suitable land and buildings								
	35 Other								
	Total this section								
Labour factors	36 Availability, quality and reliability of all levels of staff								
	37 Labour climate								
	38 Expatriate labour cost and availability								
	39 Mandatory costs (minimum wages, fringe benefits, etc.)								
	40 Other								
	Total this section								
Tax factors	41 Rates								
	42 'Morality' (fairness)								
	43 Long-term trends								
	44 Incentives								
	45 Treaties								
	46 Other								
	Total this section								
Capital factors	47 Local availability, cost and terms								
	48 Availability of efficient banking system								
	49 Home country attitudes to source of capital								
	50 Other								
	Total this section								
Business methods factors	51 General ethics								
	52 State of development of the marketing system								
	53 Normal profit structure								
	54 Local competition								
	55 Other								
	Total this section								

Screen 3 Specific factors influencing the company and its products or services (key success factors)									
Factors	Item	Item weight	Country A		Country B			Country N	
			Score	Total	Score	Total		Score	Total
Firm- or industry-specific factors critical to the success of the product or service									
Total this section									
Final total									

Activity 6

Review the screening tool on the above pages. Then, on a separate piece of paper and considering your own company's prospect for expansion abroad, do the following exercises.

(a) Apply Screen 1 to the countries of the EU. How many countries have you eliminated? Why?

(b) Choose the most important item from each group of factors in Screen 2. How much weight would you give to each of these factors? Why?

(c) List five categories of data that might be included in Screen 3. How would you weight each of these data items? Why?

Comment

Again we are using the Open University Business School (OUBS) as the company and the MBA as the product.

(a) Since the Single European Market was created, the EU is really an extension of OUBS's domestic market. With the exception of product acceptability, none of the eliminating factors listed was relevant to the OUBS's MBA. There is no real difficulty in the acceptability of the product we provide (English language, UK higher-degree awarding, distance-taught management education) on any of the grounds listed. You will notice a bit of verbal gymnastics in our product definition, however. By describing our product as based in the English language and UK higher-degree awarding, we create for ourselves certain expectations about the customers we choose to target. Had we decided that our product was simply 'distance-taught management education at Master's level', we would certainly have increased the potential scope of students that we could hope to attract. We might, however, have exceeded our areas of distinctive competence and created difficulties for ourselves in the countries of the EU. For example, if we described our product simply as Master's-level, distance-taught management education, we would have had to conform to the rules of accreditation established by each country's ministry of education. There are two important points here. First, the ways in which you define your products impinge upon their acceptability. Should you find that your current product description is unacceptable in many otherwise attractive markets, it might be advisable to modify the product description and try again. The second point is related to the first. By choosing to define our product in a certain way, we have placed specific limitations upon ourselves. We have limited those whom we are willing to deal with and the ways in which we will interact with the host government. Our product definition has resulted from a conscious consideration of our resources, our distinctive competence, and our potential customer group. This is a common practice among firms. Our product has to be defined at some point, and for this exercise the definition is needed as a base. Note, however, that this product focus is antithetical to the marketing notion that customers drive product design. The Marketing unit later in the course discusses this issue in greater detail.

(b) We chose seven items, and gave them the weights shown in Table 3. In this process, note that we assigned weights based on a specific logic that was important to our business.

Table 3	
Item	Weight
8 Balance of economy	7
15 Conflict between social groups	5
26 Intellectual property law	8
(We omitted 'geographic factors' because none seemed appropriate to the OUBS)	
36 Availability, quality and reliability of staff	10
41 Tax rates	8
48 Availability of efficient banking system	4
52 State of development of the marketing system	9

Our logic for these weights was that tutor quality (item 36) was critical to the successful delivery of our product and therefore the most important issue for us. The number of managers in a country, and the degree to which they want/need to learn what we teach, impinged upon our weightings for items 8, 15 and 52. The need to protect our investment led to the weights for items 26 and 41, and the ability to get our bills paid and our money out affected our weighting for item 48. Note that we thought items 26 and 41 were twice as important to us as item 48.

The important thing to point out here is not the weights we gave items. Neither is it the reasons why we chose specific weights. Instead, we suggest that you found you wanted different information from that in this checklist. Like us, you may have also found that some of the items listed had no effect on your analysis. You should note that this checklist is only a guide. It serves as a way to structure the process of thinking. It is here to be added to, subtracted from, and modified to fit your own company.

(c) The part of the system which is specifically designed to allow you to add items that are of interest to your company is Screen 3. We mentioned some of the issues we might want to include in this screen earlier (page 36), so will not comment on them again now. To restate the point above, it is important that you review the list with an eye to the information you will need to choose those countries in which you have the greatest opportunity to succeed, thus reducing opportunity cost. No checklist can be right for every circumstance.

Step 4: Conduct detailed market research locally

When you have completed steps 1 to 3, you will probably have narrowed the list down to a manageable number of countries that your company might enter. Often, the scores cluster in a way that indicates a few clear choices. At other times, you will simply have to decide how many countries you want to invest additional time and money in to get the detailed information you need. The options for you at this point probably require that you send managers to the target country (the grand tours suggested earlier). Either a few go with specific briefs, or only one might go with the goal of contacting a market research company based in the host country to buy detailed advice. In either instance, it could be well that the managers involved have a clear understanding of your company's goals, and have to keep to both time and cost budgets.

Issue monitoring

The second (and probably more common) situation in which firms find themselves is that they have already started operations in one or more host countries. The task of reviewing and assessing the political circumstances in a company's operating areas is somewhat different from the task for a company not yet operating outside its home country. In this case, a technique called *issue monitoring* is used. The purpose of issue monitoring is to determine the issues that are likely to impinge upon the continuing activities of the company in each country where it operates. A sound issue management system will also enable the company to assess whether issues are converging at regional or global level.

Activity 7

Please turn to the Reader article by Sharp, 'Business environment assessment', and read it now. When you have finished reading, return to the comment below.

Comment

Daniel Sharp worked for the Xerox Corporation, which is in the information business. Xerox has a strong corporate affairs unit, and takes issue monitoring seriously at all levels within the organization. Xerox has modified and extended the system since Sharp wrote the Reader article, but the central ideas in his article are still in use. Note that some features of the suggestions Sharp makes will probably have to be altered a little to fit the structure of your company, especially those that relate to the flow of the information generated by the system.

The most important point to make about this system is that it requires managers in the company to be aware of political issues as they develop. By making use of the knowledge bases of the firm's local managers (who often have solid information and sound intuition concerning the conditions in the country in which they operate), a company can then capitalize on its information advantage.

A recap

To conclude Section 3.1, we want to recap what we think are the key points. We have emphasized that all managers in your company must be aware of and involved in constantly assessing the political environment in which they operate. We have pointed out that an understanding of the political situation is essential to the extent that it impinges upon your company's decision-making process. We suggested two related, but different, systems of data gathering and analysis (political risk analysis and issue monitoring), depending on whether your company is currently in, or deciding to enter, a new country. Both of these methods contain prescriptions for the kinds of information that might be needed and the types of process that might be put into place to manage the data gathering and analysis.

But understanding the nature of the political environment is not enough: firms need to manage the risk and opportunity associated with political action. In the remainder of Section 3, we explore two general strategies that will help you to understand the management of political opportunity and risk.

3.2 BUFFER: DECISIONS THAT LIMIT YOUR EXPOSURE TO RISK

As we discuss in the Strategy unit, any company will want to consider how to minimize adverse political action. This notion is called 'buffering'. Two broad strategies exist to buffer political risk. We should point out, however, that only rarely are all tactics of one strategy used exclusively. Often, tactics from both strategies are used in conjunction with one another in well thought-out plans.

The first strategy, *integration with the host country*, is based on the idea that the company should try to become (and be seen to be) a 'local' company. By doing this, it is more likely to blend into the business community of the host community, and thus escape special notice and treatment.

Companies might employ a local workforce, borrow money from local banks and other sources of capital, and involve local interests in their business as much as possible. They might form joint ventures with local companies, which has implications for both partners. For instance, if the company recruits many local people and owes a great deal of money to local banks, its financial losses, bankruptcy or withdrawal will directly affect those people and those banks. Also, if it is forced to fold or to give up operations and leave the country, the assets and capital, which are largely owned by the local people, will be lost. Policies such as these would either act as a deterrent or prevent the local government from taking actions that might ultimately hurt its own people and institutions.

The second strategy, *avoidance of exposure*, is designed to limit a company's risk in host countries as far as possible. In this strategy, modes of entry and operation are designed so that the company's assets, both human and capital, are all located beyond the reach of adverse governmental activity. Key decision-making processes, research and development, and the acquisition of capital all take place outside the host country. The company might want to strictly control its internal market. If, for example, a company is using the country as a source of supply, it might check that no other company is operating downstream of the supply activity in the host country, and that relationships between supplier and customer are based on contracts between two separate legal entities. In the event that the company is forced to close down, no other firm can then serve as a market for the supplies produced in the host country. The company could also be clear that it will retain its legal rights over brand names and trademarks in the host country. If it is nationalized, neither the new company nor any other firm will be allowed to use its brand name. In countries with good market prospects but high risk, one way of avoiding risk is to use licensing, franchising, management or know-how contracts instead of wholly owned subsidiaries.

3.3 INFLUENCE: ADJUSTING THE BALANCE OF POWER

If your firm is already present in a country, the options for buffering are more constrained. The tactics for limiting exposure are usually more difficult (and often costly) to apply after entry. You could move steadily towards integration with the host country, and this is often part of the natural process as companies grow and develop in a country. Efforts to rush this process, however, can be costly and inadvisable on strategic grounds. What, then, can a company do to minimize the degree to which political action negatively affects it in these circumstances?

We suggested earlier that the balance of power between a company and political entities is not one-sided. In practice, however, companies need to find ways constantly to remind political decision makers of this fact. We have argued throughout this unit that (because of the diversity of political actors) this process is more difficult for international enterprises than for domestic ones. Sections 1 and 2 suggested some of the array of political, economic and social organizations that may have to be dealt with. As you may recall, the list includes not only individual host countries but also the company's home country and selected regional and global organizations. Each of these is a legitimate target for the exercise of political influence.

The process by which companies exercise influence with political decision makers is called 'lobbying'. This word may wrongly conjure up the stereotypical image of smoke-filled corridors, expensively tailored clothing, and smooth-talking professionals with good networks of contacts. The reality is that lobbying is a legitimate and desirable part of the political decision-making process in most nations.

When we use the term 'lobbying', we are talking about a complex process that helps managers to understand the political issues of the day, to communicate the views of the company to those with influence in the decision-making process and, if (and only if) necessary, to exercise the countervailing power of the company.

The lobbying process is organized in different ways by firms. In some it is done exclusively at the top level with input from legal departments, corporate affairs personnel, and government relations specialists. In others, the process involves managers with line or staff responsibility. For example, one of the contributors to this course is a manager in a pharmaceutical company. He chairs an EU-wide committee of representatives from his industry whose main purpose is to influence the decision-making process of the EU. Trade associations and chambers of commerce too often have a formal role in lobbying government and quasi-governmental organizations.

Most firms make use of their chief executive officer and non-executive directors in the influence process. Their range of contacts is often critical to the success of the process. Some firms with significant presence in host countries employ public relations and corporate affairs professionals on their central staff. Others, with different goals, may delegate the corporate affairs process to local operating units. Yet other firms entrust the process to the marketing director, who might use consultants. Other companies involve themselves with trade associations. Some limit their corporate affairs functions to part of the responsibilities of their senior managers. No matter how lobbying is organized, there are certain general stages that companies follow. These include monitoring political issues, informing decision makers and negotiating outcomes. All of this takes place in the context of a clear understanding of the political process as set out in Section 1.

Understanding the political system

We argued in Section 1 that it is critical to understand the structure, processes and relationships between those political groups whose actions affect your company. This quest for understanding should not be limited to the corporate affairs unit or the senior management of the company. Every manager, no matter what their function or level in the company, needs to be aware of the political processes that will impinge upon the company. The only other point to emphasize here is that companies must gain this understanding of all groups that exercise political influence over them. You should, therefore, learn about relevant regional and global organizations. Increasingly, for example, the EU is becoming the major regulator of commercial activity for companies operating within it. Ignorance of its processes and structure will be an increasing handicap for managers.

Miller (1990) discusses the issue, and a summary of his key points is given in Table 4.

Table 4 Questions to answer that will help you understand the political system of a host country
1 Who makes decisions which affect my company?
2 Who influences these decision makers?
3 To whom do we put our company's case?
4 What is the best way we can make our case?
5 How do we obtain access to decision makers?
6 What is the best way to monitor the government?
7 When is the right time to monitor, to talk, to argue or to pressure?

Monitoring issues

We suggested in Section 3.1 that companies need to monitor the political environment in those countries in which they are operating or intend to operate. We will again remind you that this process is not limited to senior managers and corporate affairs people. No matter what your function in a company, political action is likely to impinge upon your performance in your job. The more aware you are of impending change, the better you will be able to do your job in the company.

Informing decision makers and negotiating outcomes

For political bodies, one of the most important benefits of lobbying is that it provides decision makers with a rich variety of information that otherwise they would not have access to. A Euro MP has stated that, without lobbyists, she would have to employ an army of researchers to gain the same level of understanding of the issues that she got free from interested parties and that, even if she did employ 'impartial' researchers, much of the information she gained would have been either unavailable or filtered in some way by those providing it. In summary, she said: 'on the whole, lobbyists are a positive asset to our decision making.'

The point we are trying to make here is that, contrary to a commonly accepted view that lobbying is a process aimed at 'special pleading', the reality is that, without it, political decision makers could not do their jobs as well. Firms are in a unique position to provide political decision makers with information on the current situations that their industries face, and to make assessments concerning the potential effects of proposed political actions on their industries. The lobbying process therefore aids and strengthens the political decision-making process. Companies sometimes make the mistake of meeting a top minister, for example, when it might be more useful to talk with officials responsible for drafting legislation that might affect the company.

We should remind you here of the analogy made in Section 1 between the political decision-making process and industrial buying behaviour. The process of informing decision makers also contains an element of negotiating with them. It is therefore important that the firm interacts with the most appropriate people in the process.

One final point needs to be made here. Each political institution is set within a culture where certain values and behaviours are deemed appropriate. The Culture unit demonstrates the need to understand these values and behaviours in order for you to be effective in the negotiating process. The Marketing unit highlights some negotiating issues in more detail. For now, it is important for you to recognize that each country not only has different systems and processes, but also different interpersonal and cultural rules that must be followed.

3.4 CONCLUSION

This section of the unit looked at what a company can do to manage its exposure to political action. First we looked at what you and your company need to do to understand the political features of your environment. We looked in detail at two techniques for this. The first, applied before entry into a new country, was political risk analysis. The second was issue monitoring. We next suggested that it was possible for a company to buffer its exposure to political action using techniques that would allow it to become integrated with the host society, or to avoid exposure almost entirely. Finally, we turned to the issue of influencing political decision makers. Here we suggested that two important preconditions must exist before influence can be exercised. The first is that you understand the political process of the political actor you are trying to influence. The second is that you have developed an active issue-monitoring system within your own company. Finally, we suggested that lobbying political decision makers was a valuable activity performed by firms.